I CAN READ IT ALL BY MYSELF

Beginner Books

Originally published by Random House, Inc., as two books—in 1960 under the title *Bennett Cerf's Book of Riddles* and in 1961 under the title *More Riddles* by Bennett Cerf.

www.randomhouse.com/kids

Library of Congress Cataloging-in-Publication Data

Cerf, Bennett, 1898–1971.
[Book of riddles]
Riddles and more riddles! / by Bennett Cerf ; illustrated by Debbie Palen.
p. cm. — (Beginner books)
First work originally published: New York : Beginner books, 1960; 2nd work originally published: New York : Beginner books, 1961.
Contents: Book of riddles — More riddles.
SUMMARY: A collection of riddles, such as "When is a cook bad? When she beats an egg," and "What kind of coat should be put on when it is wet? A coat of paint."
ISBN 0-679-88970-1 (trade) — ISBN 0-679-98970-6 (lib. bdg.)
1. Riddles, Juvenile. [1. Riddles. 2. Jokes.] I. Palen, Debbie, ill. II. Cerf, Bennett, 1898–1971. More riddles. III. Title. IV. Title: More riddles. V. Series.
PN6371.5.C38 1999 818'.5202—dc21 99-20133

Printed in the United States of America   10 9 8 7 6 5 4 3

Riddles
and More Riddles!

By Bennett Cerf
Illustrated by Debbie Palen

Where will a cat be when

the lights go out?

In the dark.

BEGINNER BOOKS®

A Division of Random House, Inc.

What should you do when you see a big lion?

Hope the big lion does not see you.

What is the last thing you take off when you go to bed?

You take your feet off the floor.

What gets lost every
time you stand up?

Your lap.

Why do birds fly south?

Because it is too far to walk.

What do giraffes have that
no other animals have?

Little giraffes.

Why did the firefighter
wear red suspenders?

To keep his pants up.

Why did the little boy
throw the clock
out the window?

Because he wanted to see time fly.

What time is it when an

elephant sits on a fence?

Time to get a new fence.

CRUNCH!

What did the big firecracker say to the little firecracker?

"My pop is bigger than your pop."

Why does a cow go over a hill?

Because a cow can't go under a hill.

Why do white sheep eat so much more than black sheep?

Because there are so many more white sheep.

What is a bird after she is four days old?

Five days old.

What holds up a bank?

Bad people.

What did the pig say when a man got him by the tail?

The pig said, "This is the end of me."

What dog keeps the best time?

A watchdog.

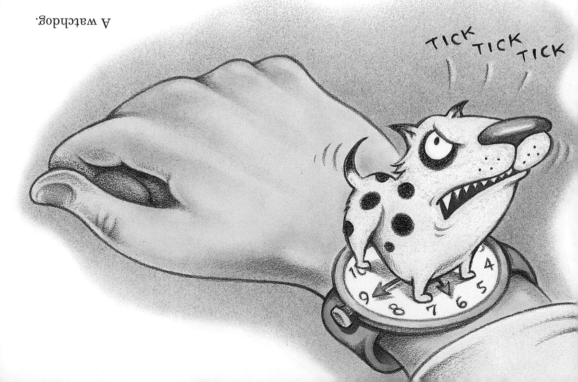

What is big and red
and eats rocks?

A big red rock eater.

How many balls of string would it take to reach the moon?

Just one. But it would have to be a big one.

Why does a hen lay eggs?

Because if she let them drop, they would break.

What makes more noise
than a cat stuck in a tree?

Two cats stuck in a tree.

What kind of animal has a head like a cat
and a tail like a cat, but is not a cat?

A kitten.

If you drop a white hat
into the Red Sea,
what will it become?

Wet.

Name five things that have milk in them.

1.

2.

3.

4.

5.

Who always goes to bed
with his shoes on?

A horse.

When is a cook bad?

When she beats an egg.

Why is an egg
not like an elephant?

If you do not know, I would not
want to send you to get eggs.

For what man should you
always take off your hat?

The barber.

When will a net hold water?

When the water turns to ice.

Our hen can lay an egg four inches long. Can you beat that?

Yes. With an eggbeater.

What is the best way to keep
a skunk from smelling?

Hold her nose.

What is the best way
to make pants last?

Make the
coat first.

What is white,
has just one horn,
and gives milk?

A milk truck.

What kind of animal eats with his tail?

All kinds of animals eat with their tails.
They can't take them off.

What is the hardest thing about learning to ride a bicycle?

The thing you fall on.

Why did the little girl put ice in her father's bed?

Because she liked cold pop.

What is the best
thing to put
into a pie?

Your teeth.

What comes all the
way to a house but
never goes in?

The steps.

Why does a giraffe
eat so little?

Because a giraffe can make
a little go a long way.

What horse can fly like a bird?

A horse fly.

Why does a cook always put on a tall white hat?

To cover his head.

What has...Two legs like a cowboy? Two eyes like a cowboy? Two hands like a cowboy? Looks just like a cowboy? But is not a cowboy?

A picture of a cowboy.

Can you drop a full glass
and not spill any water?

Yes, when the glass is full of milk.

What looks just like
half a loaf of bread?

The other half a loaf of bread.

What goes up when the

rain comes down?

An umbrella.

When should you give
elephant milk to a baby?

When the baby is an elephant.

What can fall down
and never get hurt?

Snow can fall down
and never get hurt.

Which will burn longer:

the candles on the birthday cake of a boy,

or the candles on the birthday cake of a girl?

No candles burn longer. They all burn shorter.

What kinds of animals can jump higher than a house?

All kinds of animals. Houses cannot jump.

What bird can't fly as high as you can jump?

A bird in a cage.

When is a boy not a boy?

When he turns into a store.

What kind of dog has no tail?

A hot dog.

What is the first thing you put in a garden?

Your foot.

How many lions can you put in an empty cage?

One. After that, the cage is not empty.

What kind of coat
should be put on
when it is wet?

A coat of paint.

When can three big
women go out under
one little umbrella
and not get wet?

When it is not raining.

Why does a stork stand on one leg?

Because if she took two legs off the ground, she would fall down.

What is the best way to get something out from under an elephant?

Wait for the elephant to go away.

What is the best way to catch a fish?

Have someone throw it to you.

What sings, has four legs,
is yellow, and weighs
1,000 pounds?

Two 500-pound canaries.

What is the best way to make
a fire with two sticks?

Make sure one of the sticks is a match.

Why does a baby pig
eat so much?

To make a hog of himself.

When should you put a saddle
on a horse backward?

When you want to see where you have been.

I CAN READ IT ALL BY MYSELF

Beginner Books